Roy Apps

The Saga of
Leif Erikson:
Outlaw's Son

Illustrated by Alan Marks

Macdonald Young Books

GREENLAND

ICELAND .

NORTH
AMERICA

GREAT
BRITAIN

NORWAY

SWEDEN

IRELAND

VINLAND
(the 'Land of No-Frost')

EUROPE

AFRICA

THE YEAR 970
LEFT TO THE WOLVES

On a frosty February night, in a wooden
hut just above a Norwegian fjord*, a
woman known as Gudrid gave birth to
a son.

There was no rejoicing. The baby was
a puny-looking thing and as pale as a
trussed-up chicken waiting for the spit.

The father, known as Erik the Red,
turned his head away in disappointment
and disgust.

* A long, narrow arm of sea between high cliffs

5

"You know what you must do," he muttered to his wife's slave-woman.

The family's dog whined in the corner.

Straightaway, the slave-woman grabbed the baby from its sobbing mother and stepped out of the hut. Only then did she wrap the baby in her cloak.

She walked towards the mountainside.

The dog went with her.

Then the slave-woman placed the baby by a ragged gorse bush on the wildest part of the mountain.

She left it there for the wolves.

As is the Viking custom.

She called the dog to follow her back to their mistress's hut. The dog growled and lay down with its paws outstretched. It would not follow her. "The Lord keep you," she whispered, for unlike her Viking mistress, she was a Christian.

Next morning, old Olaf, the blind bone-carver, heard the sound of crying coming from a gorse bush.

He found the baby, hungry but warm enough, snuggled like a young pup under the belly of the dog.

Neither dog nor baby
had been troubled by wolves.

Gudrid wept when the old man brought in the baby.

"It is the will of the gods that the child shall live," declared Erik. "Let him be known by the name Leif."

This is the saga of Leif Erikson, known as the Lucky One.

2
Outlaws!

Leif continued to grow in strength. He was worked hard by his father; ploughing in the spring, gathering gulls' eggs in the summer, laying up wood in the autumn and mending and making tools in the winter.

Erik was never comfortable in his son's company; this boy whom the gods had decreed should live.

During the long, dark months, Erik would sit by the fire and tell his wife Gudrid a saga told to him by his father, Knud. It was a saga of a land that was so warm there was no frost; a land surrounded by a sea that was as blue as the transparent sapphire gemstones brought back by the eastern traders.

Leif, who should have been sleeping, listened and heard.

One night in his excitement, he said out loud, "When I am grown, I shall sail to the Land of No-Frost!"

Erik laughed. A cruel, mocking laugh that left its scar on Leif's heart.

Erik was called the Red for red was the colour of his temper.

One autumn day, he argued with Ivar Bent-Nose over the price of a Celtic slave. He brought his axe down on Ivar Bent-Nose's head, killing him with a single blow.

The members of the *Althing** met in judgement and ruled that Erik the Red, his family and his oath-friends should be outlawed.

As is the Viking custom.

* Viking law court

12

Erik and his family and friends
sailed west.

"Perhaps we shall find the Land of
No-Frost," thought Leif. But they only
managed to sail as far as Iceland.

Although the land here was even harsher than in Norway and the winters colder and darker, Leif was happy.

He made friends with
Thorvald and Freya,
the children of
Thorgeir Grey-Beard.

During the long dark winter days
he told them a saga.

It was the saga told to him by his father, Erik the Red; which in turn had been told to him by *his* father, Knud. It was a saga of a land that was so warm there was no frost; a land surrounded by a sea that was as blue as the transparent sapphire gemstones that were sometimes brought back by the eastern traders.

"When I am grown, I shall sail to the Land of No-Frost," said Leif.

Freya smiled at Leif: a smile which told him that she, if no one else, believed him.

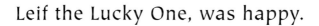

Leif the Lucky One, was happy.

THE YEAR 983
THE ISLAND AT THE
EDGE OF THE WORLD

3

One fine spring day, Erik argued with
Thorgeir Grey-Beard over some sheep
pasture. He lunged at Thorgeir Grey-
Beard with his sword and killed him.

The members of the Althing met in judgement and ruled that Erik the Red, his family and his oath-friends should be outlawed for three winters and three summers.

As is the Viking custom.

One night Leif woke to the sound of scuffling outside the hut.

"Leif the Lucky One,
is that you?"

Leif's friend, Thorvald
Thorgeirson stood there,
his sword at the ready.

"Listen to me, for I do not intend to
stay here long. I have no quarrel with
you, friend, but I must warn you that
my uncles, cousins and I have sworn
oaths to avenge my father's death.
Your house will be torched tomorrow
night and anyone sleeping there will
perish by fire or by the sword."

It is the Viking law that anyone may
kill an outlaw without fear of punishment.

At dawn, Erik the Red, his family and his oath-friends sailed west again.

"This time we must surely find the Land of No-Frost," thought Leif.

They sailed for many weeks, but the land they eventually found was cold and desolate.

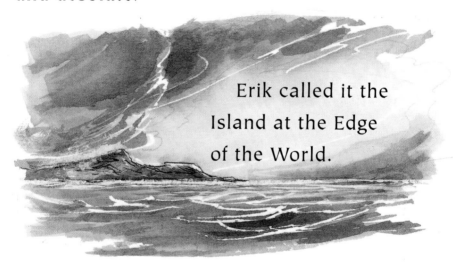

Erik called it the Island at the Edge of the World.

After three hard winters and three summers that were little better, Erik called together his family, his household and his oath-friends.

"Now that my banishment-time has been served and I am an outlaw no longer, we shall sail east, back to Iceland."

"We have no land in Iceland," protested Gudrid.

"I shall bring people from Iceland back here with us. With more help, this land can be tilled and the seas can be properly fished."

THE YEAR 986
4 ERIK'S CRUEL TRICK

"How will you persuade people here to sail to the Island at the Edge of the World?" asked Leif, as they finally hauled the longship up onto the Icelandic shore.

"You'll see," said Erik, laughing.

That afternoon, he addressed a large gathering. Leif the Lucky One was at his side.

"I Erik the Red, my family and oath-friends have sailed far. We have discovered a new land."

Leif waited for his father to say,
"I have called this new land the Island
at the Edge of the World."

Instead, he heard him say, "I have
called this new land *Green*land, for it is
a green, warm and pleasant land. Who
amongst you wishes to sail back there
with us?"

He makes the Island at the Edge
of the World sound like the Land of
No-Frost, thought Leif.

An excited murmur ran through the crowd. Erik looked pleased with himself.

But Leif felt uncomfortable and embarrassed by his father's cruel trick.

He left his father talking to the crowd and went in search of news of his friend Thorvald Thorgeirson.

He found Thorvald's sister Freya weaving cloth. Three winters and two summers had turned her into a handsome and self-possessed young woman.

"Thorvald set off
with a raiding party
to England last week,"
she told Leif.

"And you, Freya?"
asked Leif, pointedly.

"I tend the land
here with my husband,
Snorri Svaldson."

Leif swallowed hard.

Freya said, "And
you, Leif the Lucky
One, have you found
your Land of
No-Frost?"

Leif told Freya about the Island at the Edge of the World and of the cruel trick his father was playing on the people of the village.

He left not long after. On the track he passed an excited young man running over the fields. It was Snorri Svaldson.

"Freya," he cried at the top of his voice, "gather up your wool and round up our pigs! For tomorrow we sail to the warm and lush pastures of Greenland with Erik the Red!"

Of the twenty-five ships that sailed from Iceland, only fourteen completed the journey to Greenland.

Erik, the chief, his wife Gudrid and Leif Erikson, the Lucky One, were safe.

Also safe were Snorri Svaldson and his wife, Freya, who was expecting their child. Safe too was the old sailor and raider, Bjarni Sea-Tamer; it was said he knew almost as much of this world as the gods themselves.

The winter was hard. Those who had sailed with Erik had known hard winters back in Iceland, but nothing like this.

The icy air made you weep and then the wind froze the tears on your cheeks.

When people looked Erik the Red in the face, there was anger in their eyes.

So, two slaves were sacrificed to win the help of Freyr, the harvest god.

As is the Viking custom.

"Spring will be better,"
said Erik, uneasily.

It wasn't.

The ground did not thaw. Seed could not be planted. The winter feed was finished and the animals starved.

The people ate fish.

One bitterly cold night as they sat round the fire, Bjarni Sea-Tamer told Leif of a land he had once spotted, when his ship had been blown westward.

"The Land of No-Frost!" murmured Leif, excitedly. "Bjarni Sea-Tamer, you saw the Land of No-Frost!"

Old Bjarni Sea-Tamer said nothing, but sat quite still looking into the glowing embers of the fire.

Leif told his friend Snorri Svaldson who said, "We must sail west. We must find the Land of No-Frost!"

They told Erik the Red, who said,
"Nobody is sailing anywhere! We need
all the help we can get here."

He looked his son Leif in the eye.
"Rid yourself of those childish notions
about a Land of No-Frost," he snarled.
He pointed to the distant horizon.
"What has been handed down
to us is this. All that man will
find beyond this sea is
Utgard, the Land of the
Frost-Giants."

Snorri Svaldson said, "If you stay here more than a week longer, Erik, the only journey you'll ever make is to the Other World. There are many who seek to spill your blood for tricking us so."

Erik the Red had seen enough of the people's faces to know that Snorri Svaldson's warning was a timely one. With little enthusiasm, he prepared to sail west with his son, Leif, the Lucky One.

It was while he was checking the timbers on his *knorr** that the mast fell, smashing his leg.

Some said it was a deliberate act by an avenging neighbour. Others said it was simply the work of the gods.

* Small Viking boat

THE YEAR 990
VINLAND

Leif Erikson, the Lucky One, prepared to set sail west.

He took Snorri Svaldson with him as his ship-brother, together with a dozen other men who were all experienced sea-raiders.

"May *Thor** guard you," Gudrid whispered to her son.

"May Thor guard you," echoed Leif.

* Viking God of Thunder

Erik the Red, the Chief, said nothing, but sat on his chair, his leg heavily strapped, his face dark and brooding.

Leif watched from his boat until his father was no more than a speck on the horizon. He knew his father's life was still under threat from his angry neighbours and that he would probably not see him again.

At first, the air and the waters seemed to Leif to be getting colder and colder. There were mutterings among the men about being led over the ocean's edge to Utgard, where the Frost-Giants ruled. Leif and Snorri shut their ears to such talk.

After many days sailing, the air began to feel warmer and the sea began to look bluer.

One morning, Leif woke to find they were sailing in water the colour of the transparent sapphire gemstones that had sometimes been brought back to Norway by the eastern traders.

It did not surprise him when Snorri spotted a land mass to their *steer-board**.

"The Land of No-Frost," he whispered to himself.

* Starboard or right-hand side of a ship

Leif had never seen
grass so green,
nor leaves so lush.

"What are these?"
called Snorri, picking
some large berries that
looked as ripe as bruises.

Leif recalled how in
Norway, the eastern
traders had told how
wine was made.

"I believe these are
wild grapes," he said.
"The fruit from which
wine is made."

Leif the Lucky One renamed the Land
of No-Frost, Vinland – the land of wine.

The winter days were longer and
warmer. They ate salmon and wild boar.

The following spring they set sail
for home.

6 THE YEAR 991
HOME

The journey home was a terrible one indeed. Cruel storms battered the boat. Half the crew were drowned, among their number Snorri Svaldson.

But Thor himself watched over Leif the Lucky One.

The people had seen the knorr as it approached Greenland and knew who it must be.

Leif was first over the prow when the knorr rode up the Greenland shore.

The first person he saw was Freya.

"Freya," he said gently, taking her hand, "Snorri Svaldson, your husband and my ship-brother, is dead."

Then Freya left Leif, so that she could go back to her home to weep.

Leif turned to his mother Gudrid.

"Erik is still alive," she said. She seemed years older than when Leif had left her the previous summer. "But his leg has not healed. He will soon be making his final journey to the Other World."

"The neighbours did not kill him?"

"They thought it punishment enough for him to suffer the shame of an old man's death, a straw-bed death," muttered Gudrid.

Leif found his father lying on a straw mattress in a corner of the hut.

"It was *my* dream," sighed Erik, "to find the Land of No-Frost."

"You believed in it all along?" whispered Leif.

Erik struggled to raise his head. "But it was the will of the gods that it should be you, Leif, who made the discovery. Just as it was their will at your birth that you should live, Leif the Lucky One."

Father and son embraced.

By sunset that evening, Erik the Red was dead.

Ten days later, he was laid in his river boat. Two pigs, a hen and a slave woman were killed and put with him. Then Leif the Lucky One, the closest kinsman, set the boat ablaze.

As is the Viking custom.

The new chief spoke to the people.

"I shall leave this Land at the Edge of the World and sail, not west to Vinland, but eastwards back to Iceland. For that was the homeland I was ever happiest in and that is the homeland of my new wife, Freya."

Some chose to sail with Leif,
some did not.

Leif and Freya prospered. They
raised a large family of both sons and
daughters. Leif made many voyages
and took part in many raids.

He never returned to Vinland.
"I discovered the land where there was
no frost, where the grapes grew wild;
that was the will of the gods. I have
no need to return."

Long after he had made his last
voyage to the Other World, his
grandchildren told their children
the saga of their great-grandfather.
And they in turn told their children.
As is the Viking custom.

*This is the saga of Leif Erikson,
known as the Lucky One.*